HOWARD GOO

INVICTUS:
A PASSION

for soprano solo, tenor solo, SATB choir
and chamber orchestra

(2017)

VOCAL SCORE

FABER *ff* MUSIC

Invictus: A Passion was commissioned by St. Luke's Friends of Music for the
St. Luke's United Methodist Church Chancel Choir, Houston, Texas,
Sid Davis, Director of Music and Fine Arts.

It was first performed on 25 March 2018 in St Luke's United Methodist Church,
Houston, Texas, by the St Luke's United Methodist Church Chancel Choir, conducted by
Howard Goodall CBE, with soloists Devon E. Jones and Ryan Jones.

It was recorded for CD release on Coro Records by soloists from The Sixteen
(Kirsty Hopkins [soprano] and Mark Dobell [tenor]), the Choir of Christ Church Cathedral,
Oxford and The Lanyer Ensemble conducted by Stephen Darlington.

Duration: c. 55 mins

Texts

Æmelia Lanyer née Bassano; Christina Georgina Rossetti; Ella Wheeler Wilcox;
Frances Ellen Watkins Harper; William Wilberforce; The Bible (Lamentations of Jeremiah;
Psalm 142; John 20:1); Antiphon for Maundy Thursday; William Ernest Henley;
A.E. Housman; Isaac Watts; W.B. Yeats; George Herbert (English & Latin)

Instrumentation

Soprano saxophone in E♭
2 Horns in F
Piano
Organ*
Double string quartet
Double bass

*or digital keyboard if a tuned pipe organ is unavailable.

Parts available on hire from the publishers (hire@fabermusic.com)

To buy Faber Music publications or to find out about the full range of titles available
please contact your local music retailer or Faber Music sales enquiries:

Faber Music Limited, Burnt Mill, Elizabeth Way, Harlow, CM20 2HX England
Tel: +44 (0)1279 82 89 82 Fax: +44 (0)1279 82 89 83
sales@fabermusic.com fabermusicstore.com

Composer's note

As with my 2008 *Eternal Light: A Requiem*, which seems to have struck a chord with performers and listeners throughout the world (it has now had over 500 live performances in at least 25 countries), in approaching the writing of a Passion setting in the 21st century, I felt it important to look at its ideas, its format and its message afresh. I couldn't simply re-run the text and the structure of the majestic 18th century Passion settings of Bach (or Handel), nor John Stainer's 'Meditation on the Sacred Passion of the Holy Redeemer', known as 'The Crucifixion', which was one of the most popular choral works of the late 19th/early 20th century. I wanted to reflect on what this story had to tell us, now.

Traditionally, the Passion narrative has taken excerpts from the Christian gospels to describe and reflect upon the final hours of the life of Jesus of Nazareth, his doubts in the Garden of Gethsemane, his trial, his public humiliation and torture, his crucifixion, his body's disappearance from the tomb and the climactic miracle of his resurrection from the dead. Whilst this final event is one uniquely adhered to by believing Christians, much of the Passion in general – persecution of the innocent, malevolent authority exerting itself against ideas that threaten and challenge, the power of a peaceful, loving humility in the face of tyranny, the facing-down of fear – holds profound universal resonance for people of many faiths and those of none. It is this universal meaning that my *Invictus: A Passion* hopes to address, so that, like *Eternal Light: A Requiem*, it might find relevance with choirs and their audiences or congregations everywhere.

One aspect of the Passion story above all others guides the choice of texts in this new piece: the role and perspective of women, in particular that of Jesus' close friend Mary Magdalene, and his mother Mary. To draw this out, I have chosen mostly (though not exclusively) female poets writing in English between the 17th and 20th centuries. The central narrative thread, for example, normally taken from St John, St Luke or St Matthew's gospels, are in this work taken from a verse version of the events written by Æmelia Lanyer née Bassano, called *Salve Deus Rex Judæorum* (Hail God, King of the Jews). This was printed in book form in 1611 (making it contemporaneous with Shakespeare's 'magical' plays, *The Winter's Tale* and *The Tempest*) and can claim to be one of the earliest, if not the first, published book in English by a female author. Lanyer is an extremely intriguing figure: a highly educated, respected woman, close to Elizabeth I and certainly known to William Shakespeare, a subject of enormous scholarly speculation as to whether she was the 'Dark Lady' alluded to in Shakespeare's sonnets, or – as some have proposed – the anonymous author of the First Folio plays herself. Recent scholarship has suggested that her family – the Bassanos, recruited in Venice to be musicians in Henry VIII's court – were in fact 'converted' Jews (converted, that is, to avoid execution, originally in Catholic Spain). In any case, her telling of the Crucifixion story is remarkable in one important respect – it is a feminist critique of the events. Its sub-headings read, 'Eve's Apologie in defence of Women', 'The Teares of the Daughters of Jerusalem' and 'The Salutation and Sorrow of the Virgine Marie'. Emphasis is therefore placed, for instance, on Pontius Pilate's wife begging for mercy for the prisoner, the injustice and pointless vengefulness of the court's proceedings with its pompous, vainglorious bullies, or on the agony of 'the two Marys' at the Cross.

Within the over-arching shape provided by excerpts from Æmelia Lanyer's extended poem, movements are interspersed by other female authors: *Gethsemane* by Ella Wheeler Wilcox (1850-1919), *Mary Magdalene and the Other Mary* by Christina Georgina Rossetti (1830-1894), and *Slave Auction* by African-American author and abolitionist campaigner Frances Ellen Watkins Harper (1825-1911). This latter poem, which forms the basis of the 2nd movement, *Lamentation*, expresses the unbearable, unimaginable pain felt by a mother seeing her child torn away from her at a slave auction. To this harrowing account are appended the words of William Wilberforce, spoken in the House of Commons on 18 April 1791, *"You may choose to look the other way but you can never say again that you did not know"*.

In the midst of appalling suffering, women so often must carry the burden of care, survival and loss. The 4th movement, *Compassion*, is inspired by the extraordinary story of Irena Sendler née Krzyżanowska, a Polish nurse and head of Żegota, the Polish Council to Aid Jews in the Second World War, whose personal interventions saved the lives of approximately 2,500 Jewish children in the Warsaw Ghetto, smuggling them to safety, acts of humanitarian bravery that eventually caused her arrest and torture by the Gestapo. She is honoured as Righteous Amongst the Nations at Yad Vashem, Jerusalem. The Latin texts of this movement are taken from the Book of Lamentations (*"My eye hath run down with streams of water, for the destruction of the daughter of my people. My enemies have chased me and caught me like a bird, without cause…"*) and from Psalm 142, the Old Testament being the meeting-point of Sendler's Catholicism and the Jewish tradition of those whose lives she saved.

For many, the greatest of all challenges to faith in the modern era has been the slaughter of innocents in successive genocides and both natural and man-made catastrophes. A 21th century Passion, therefore, cannot brush this question aside. Movement 7 reflects upon whether persistent human suffering is compatible with a loving, all-knowing deity, in a setting of A.E. Housman's agnostic exhortation to the crucified Christ, *Easter Hymn*.

As companion to Compassion, Movement 8, *The Song of Mary Magdalene: Now we are they who weep*, amalgamates Christina Rossetti's poem imagining the women in vigil at the crucified Jesus' tomb, with Isaac Watts' 1707 hymn, *When I survey the wondrous cross*, acknowledging the grief of those left to mourn.

At the fulcrum (and epilogue) of the work's architecture is William Ernest Henley's short 1875 poem, *Invictus*, a hymn-like cry of defiance in the face of terrible odds, and its final movement begins with W.B. Yeats' transcendent *The Lake Isle of Innisfree*, a vision of serenity and rebirth, written in 1893, which some have interpreted as an allegory of the afterlife. This is twinned with *The Call*, by Æmelia Lanyer's contemporary George Herbert, with its call, above all else, to embrace the inextinguishable power of love, *"Come, my Joy, my Love, my Heart: Such a Joy, as none can move: Such a Love, as none can part: Such a Heart, as joyes in love."*

Howard Goodall CBE, September 2017

Invictus: A Passion

1. Gethsemane

Æmelia Lanyer née Bassano,
Christina Georgina Rossetti,
Ella Wheeler Wilcox

Howard Goodall

1. Gethsemane

1. Gethsemane

creeps,____ and slow shad - ows____ creep.____

creeps,____ and slow shad - ows____ creep.____

12

1. Gethsemane

great salt fount of tears_____ The gard-en lies;_____ strive as you may, You can-not miss it on your

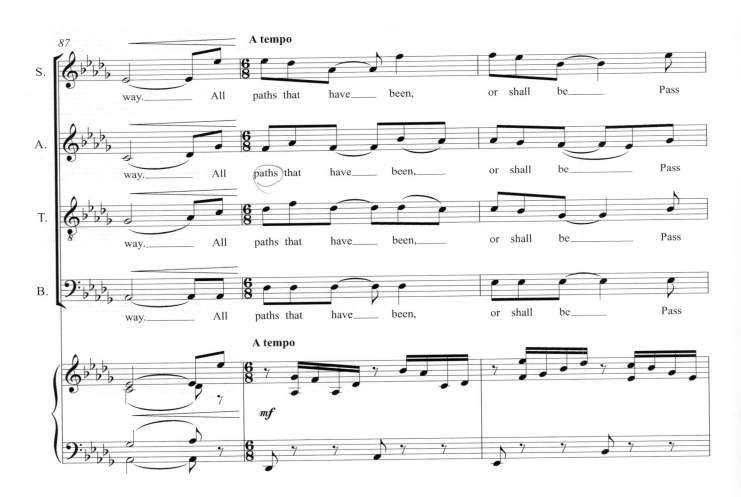

way._____ All paths that have_____ been,_____ or shall be_____ Pass

All those who jour-ney soon or late, Must pass with-in the gard-en's gate;

Must kneel a-lone in dark-ness there, And bat-tle with some fierce de-spair. God pi-ty those

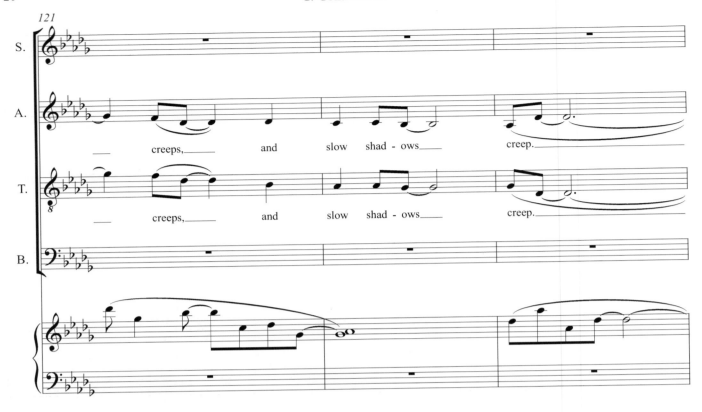

creeps,_____ and slow shad - ows_____ creep.

creeps,_____ and slow shad - ows_____ creep.

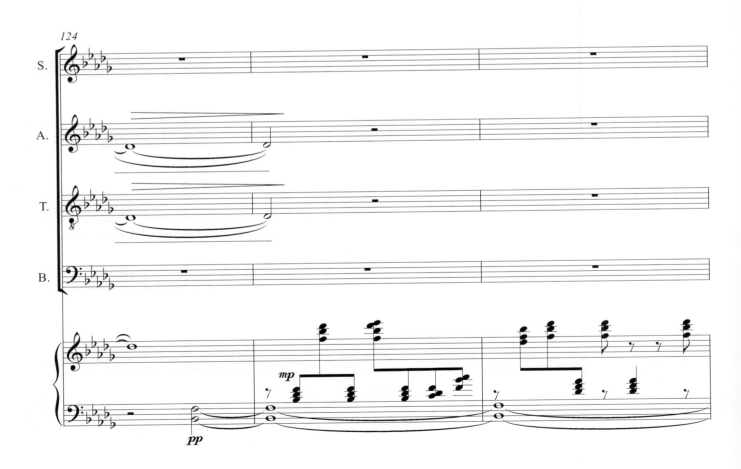

troub-led Minde,＿＿＿＿＿＿ When Heav'n and Earth were both ag - ainst thee bent?

And thou no hope, no ease, no rest could'st finde,＿＿＿＿＿＿ But must re-store that Life, which

And thou no hope, no ease, no rest could'st finde,＿＿＿＿＿＿ But must re-store that Life, which

And thou no hope, no ease, no rest could'st finde,＿＿＿＿＿＿ But must re-store that Life, which

But must re - store that Life, which

To sa-tis-fie___ for ma-ny Worlds___ of Sinne,

Whose match-less Tor-ments did but then be-gin.

2. Lamentation

Frances Ellen Watkins Harper,
William Wilberforce

The sale____ be - gan: young girls__ were there, De-

fense - less in their wretch-ed-ness, Whose stif-led sobs__ of deep de-spair__ Re -

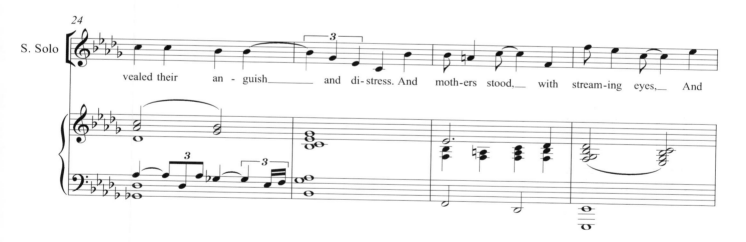

vealed their an - guish_____ and di-stress. And moth-ers stood,__ with stream-ing eyes,__ And

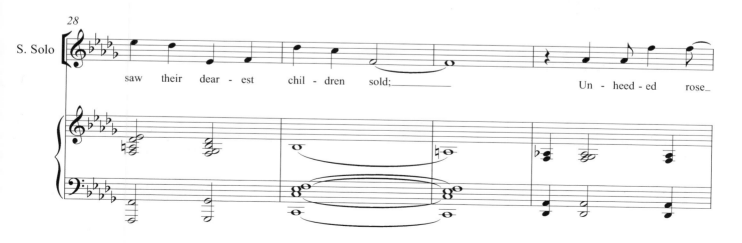

saw their dear - est chil - dren sold;_____ Un - heed - ed rose__

love and truth,___ For these in sab - le forms may dwell, Gazed on the hus - band

of her youth, With ang - uish none may paint or tell. And men, whose sole crime was their

hue,___ The im - press of their mak - er's hand.___ And frail and

3. Chorale: His Paths are Peace

Howard Goodall

Æmelia Lanyer née Bassano

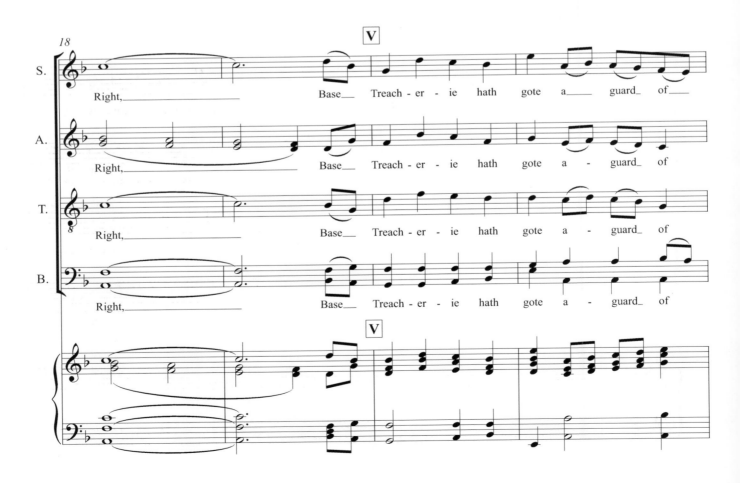

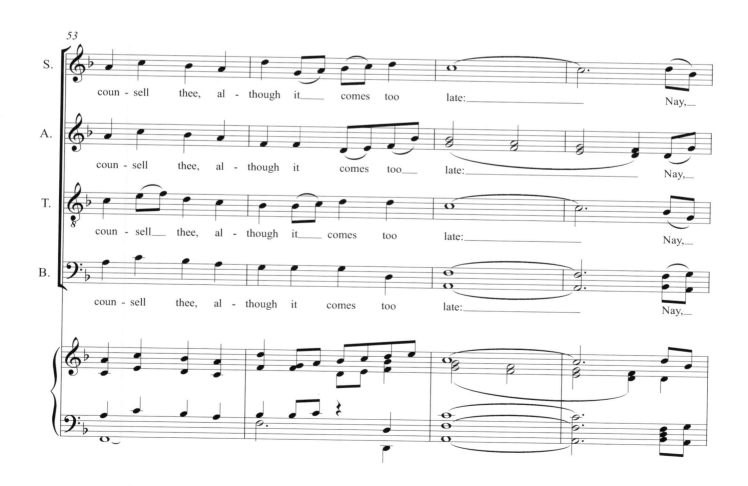

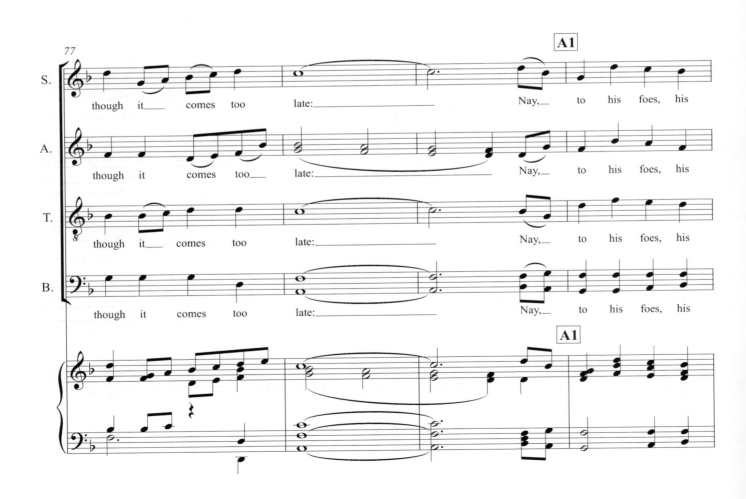

4. Compassion

Lamentations of Jeremiah 3:48, 52, 56
Psalm 142 (Vulgata Clementina)
Antiphon for Maundy Thursday

De - us___ i - bi est.___

5. Invictus

William Ernest Henley

♩ = 70

K1 *mp*

T. Solo

Out of the night that cov-ers me,___

K1

How charged with pun-ish - ments the scroll, I am the mas - ter of my

fate,_____ I am the cap - tain of my soul._____

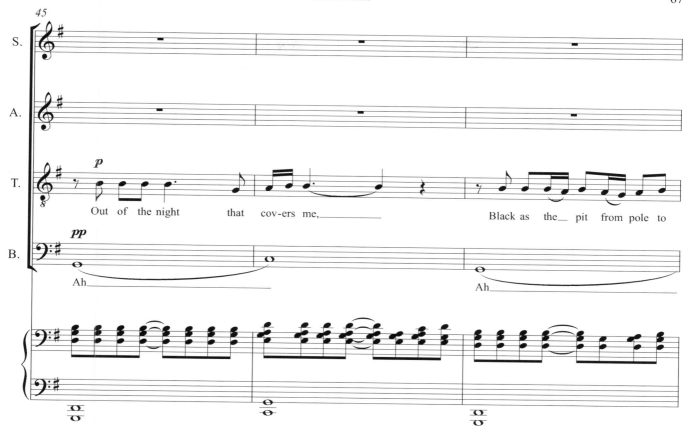

5. Invictus

74

6. Golgotha

Æmelia Lanyer née Bassano

S. O no - ble Gov-er-nour, make thou yet a pause, Doe not in in-no-cent blood im - brue thy hands;

A. O no - ble Gov-er-nour, make thou yet a pause, Doe not in in-no-cent blood im - brue thy hands;

T. O no - ble Gov-er-nour, make thou yet a pause, Doe not in in-no-cent blood im - brue thy hands;

B. O no - ble Gov-er-nour, make thou yet a pause, Doe not in in-no-cent blood im - brue thy hands;

S. ___ But heare the words of thy most wor-thy wife, Who sends to thee, to beg her Sa-viour's life.

A. ___ But heare the words of thy most wor-thy wife, Who sends to thee, to beg her Sa-viour's life,

T. ___ But heare the words of thy most wor-thy wife, Who sends to thee, her

B. ___ But heare the words of thy most wor-thy wife, Who sends to thee, to beg her Sa-viour's life,

With sharp-est thornes to pricke his bles-sed face,_____ Our joy-full sor-row, and his great-er grace.

With sharp-est thornes to pricke his bles-sed face,_____ Our joy-full sor-row, and his great-er grace.

With sharp-est thornes to pricke his bles-sed face,_____ Our joy-full sor-row, and his great-er grace.

With sharp-est thornes to pricke his bles-sed face,_____ Our joy-full sor-row, and his great-er grace.

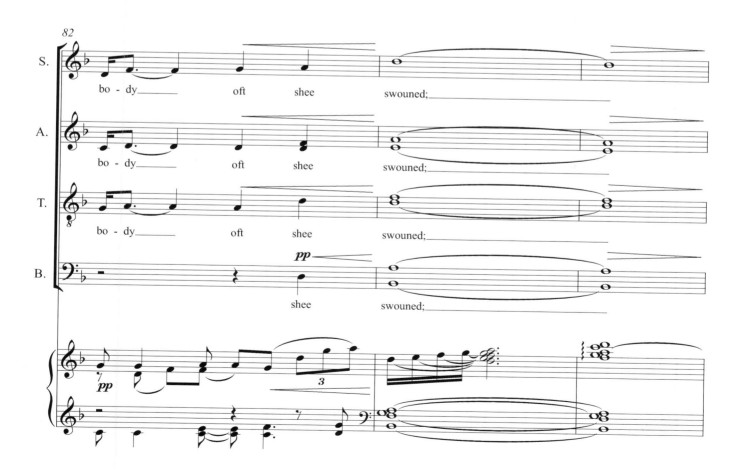

How canst thou

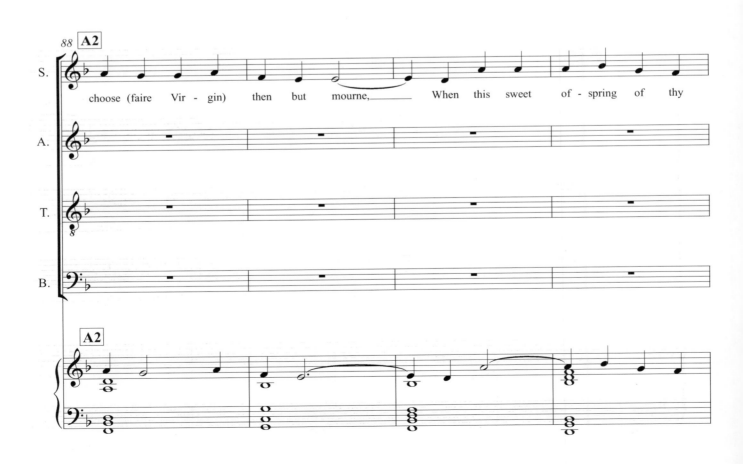

choose (faire Vir - gin) then but mourne,_____ When this sweet of - spring of thy

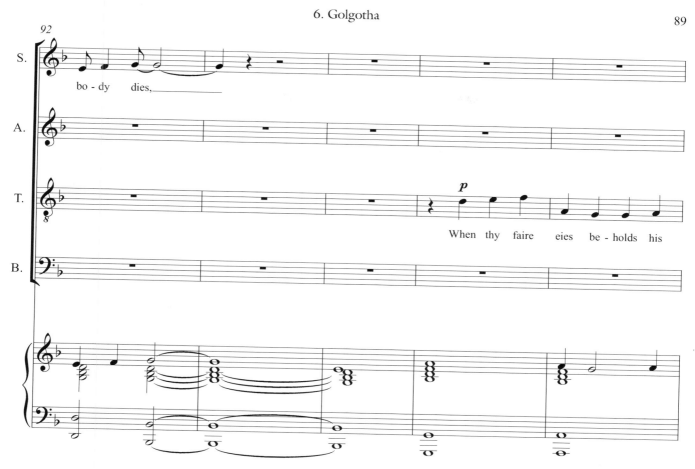

* Terrified

6. Golgotha

7. Easter Hymn

A.E. Housman

If in that Sy-rian gar-den, a-ges slain,_____ You sleep, and know not you__ are

blood-y sweat, Your cross and pas - sion and the life you gave,

Bow hi-ther out of heav'n and see and save.

But if, the grave rent and the stone rolled by,

Your cross and pas - sion and the life you gave,

Bow hi-ther out of heav'n and see and save.

Bow hi-ther out of heav'n and see and save.

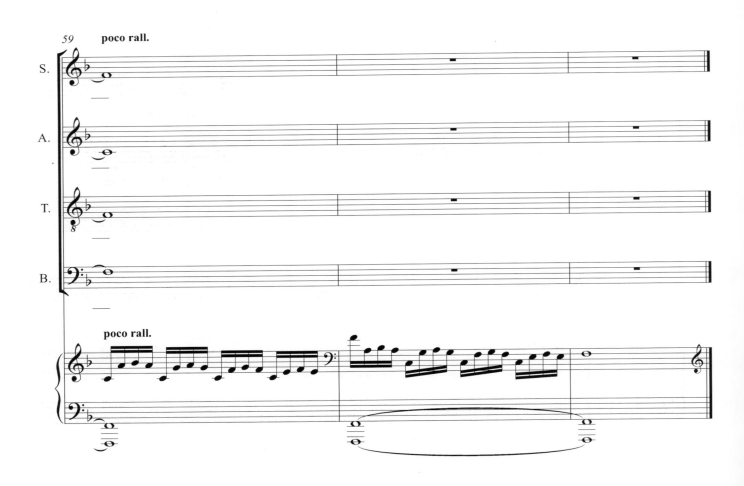

8. The Song of Mary Magdalene:
Now we are they who weep

Christina Georgina Rossetti
John 20:1
Isaac Watts

42
S. Solo
- ri - a Mag - da - - - - - le - ne
S.
- ri - a Mag - da - - - - - le - ne
A.
- ri - a Mag - - - - da - - le - ne
T.
ma - ne cum ad - huc te - ne - brae es - sent ad mo - nu - men - tum et
B.
ma - ne cum ad - huc te - ne - brae es - sent ad mo - nu - men - tum et
46
S. Solo
Ma - ri - a Mag - da - le - ne
S.
Ma - ri - a Mag - da - le - ne
A.
Ma - ri - a Mag - da - le - ne
T.
vi - det la - pi - dem sub - la - tum a mo - nu - men - to
B.
vi - det la - pi - dem sub - la - tum a mo - nu - men - to

S. Solo

S.

A.

T.

mo-nu-men-tum et vi-det la-pi-dem sub-la - tum__ a__ mo-nu-men-to__

B.

mo-nu-men-tum et vi-det la-pi-dem sub-la - tum__ a__ mo-nu-men-to__

S2

mp

S. Solo

Were the whole realm of na-ture mine, That were a

S.

A.

T.

B.

S2

W.B.Yeats
Æmelia Lanyer née Bassano
William Wilberforce
George Herbert
William Ernest Henley

9. I will arise

In - nis - free,_____ And a small ca - bin build there, of___ clay and wat - tles made:

_ I will a - rise and go now,_____ and go to

Nine bean - rows__ will I____ have there,_____ a hive__ for the hon-

- ey - bee,___ And live a - lone__ in the bee - loud glade.___   And__ shall

Drop-ping from the

have some peace__ there, for peace comes drop-ping slow,___   Drop-ping from the

9. I will arise

9. I will arise

9. I will arise